C0-DVP-940

give
your
guilt
away

give your guilt away

By J. L. Shuler

PACIFIC PRESS PUBLISHING ASSOCIATION
Mountain View, California
Omaha, Nebraska   Oshawa, Ontario

Copyright © 1972 by
Pacific Press Publishing Association
Litho in United States of America
All Rights Reserved

Library of Congress Catalog Card No. 72-79605

A Universal Problem

"Roy, did you take Sister's Indian doll out of its box?" Mother asked. She'd seen three-year-old Roy take the doll and hide it, and she wanted to give him a chance to admit what he had done. "Did you take the doll, Roy?"

He shook his head.

Who taught Roy to lie? Why did he lie before he could even talk? Why did he steal from his sister?

Roy, like the rest of us, was born with a problem—a problem called sin. We all tend to do wrong. We have a sinful nature. It is easier to disobey than obey, to make mistakes than to be perfect, to be angry than to love, to fight than to turn the other cheek, to exaggerate than to admit the truth.

Birth, life, and death are universal. So is sin. We have a double problem—the destructive things we do and our tendency to do them. Paul said of his tendency to do wrong that sin "has its lodging in me." Romans 7:20, NEB. But here is good news: God can solve your problem. He loves you, and that is why He offers you a solution. That is why He gave His Son to pay the penalty for your sins. God forgives your sins. He makes you new inside. He even shares His life—eternal life—with you if you will let Him.

"For God so loved the world, that He gave His only-begotten Son, that whosoever believeth in Him should not perish, but have everlasting life." John 3:16.

You do not have to be "good" for God to love you. Not any more than a child has to be good for his mother to love him. A mother loves her child because he is a part of herself, not because he is "good."

And God loves you just because you are you. When you sin, God does not stop loving you. His love is as strong as ever. So strong, in fact, that He gave His only Son as your Substitute and Saviour.

God loves you even while you are sinning. "But God commendeth His love toward us, in that, while we were yet sinners, Christ died for us." Romans 5:8.

God's plan is best for you. If you accept it, you will have a more abundant life—a life which is only the beginning of eternity.

If you accept God's solution, you will find out why you are here and what the purpose of your life is.

God made human beings in His own image. People were created to reveal God's righteous character. Isaiah 29:23; 43:7. But we disobeyed. We missed the goal He set for us. "Sin" means missing the mark of God's righteousness.

We do things we should not do. We say things we should not say. And often we fail to do the very things we should. A gap exists between what we are and what we ought to be. We try bridging this gap by our own efforts. We try to be good, moral, loving; but we never succeed.

God already bridged the gap for us. Through Christ's sacrifice God made a way for us to reach the goal He has set.

We have two concrete expressions of God's goodness. One, the Ten Commandments, is in written form. The other is the practical application of these commandments. It was expressed by the life of Jesus Christ.

Sin is the transgression of God's law. 1 John 3:4. "All wrongdoing is sin." 1 John 5:17, NEB.

We all violate some spiritual aspects of the Ten Commandments. We are guilty before God. Romans 3:19. Some say the commandments are not in effect now. They try to excuse themselves from sin. But a piece of lumber which is not square on each end cannot be made right by throwing away the carpenter's square. If the Ten Commandments are not in effect, then we have no ultimate authority, no guidelines. We are as confused, lost, hopeless as an inner tube in the middle of the ocean.

Sin has always been popular, and exposing it makes people angry. We do not like our faults (or sins) pointed out. We deny sin's existence, ignore it, explain it away. But no one can erase the danger of a collapsed freeway overpass by turning off the flashing yellow lights. And we cannot destroy sin by denying it exists.

We need to face three facts: (1) I am a sinner. (2) I cannot save myself from the guilt and domination of sin. (3) But Jesus can.

Christ said the Holy Spirit convicts us of sin and goodness. John 16:8. The Holy Spirit works in our intellect, will, and emotions to reveal sin. He works for all who will let Him. When we say Yes to God and allow His Spirit to convict us of sin, we will be led into a life of goodness and happiness, a life filled with personal satisfaction.

Your most important task in life is to solve your sin problem. "For what is a man profited, if he shall gain the whole world, and lose his own soul?" Matthew 16:26.

The life and death of Jesus reveal God's love for you. Let your love in return accept and obey Christ the Lord. Then you will experience His care and enter His plan for you.

Permit Jesus to solve your sin problem, and you will have the best of life: repentance (Acts 11:18), forgiveness (Colossians 1:14), a new spirituality (2 Corinthians 5:17) and Christ living His life in you (Galatians 2:20).

The law will become an actual part of you. Hebrews 8:8-10. You will have peace and joy and the acceptance of God. John 14:27; 15:11; Ephesians 1:6. Jesus will be your best friend. John 15:14. You will become an heir of God, and a joint heir with Christ. Romans 8:15-17. The Holy Spirit will comfort you and give you power. John 14:16-20. You will become perfect in Christ and receive eternal life. Colossians 1:28; 1 John 5:11.

GIVE YOUR GUILT AWAY

There is only One who can meet your need. When Peter was sinking in the sea, he prayed, "Lord, save me." Instantly there was a hand to save him. All who reach out to Him are saved.

Your eternal welfare hinges on the solution of your sin problem. If you accept God's solution, you have eternal life in Christ. And you will enter eternal happiness in heaven. If you reject His solution, you choose to suffer everlasting destruction.

The choice is yours.

Man-made Solutions

I visited a cathedral on a weekday. It was located on top of a hill. A hundred steps led to the entrance; and scores of people, climbing the stairway, knelt and prayed on each step.

Why did they pray on each step? They were trying to be "good." They thought kneeling and praying like that would make God more willing to forgive their sins.

In another city I saw men pierce their ears, lips, noses, or cheeks with skewers and walk barefoot through red-hot coals.

People lie on beds of spikes, beat themselves with whips, and torture themselves in other ways. In some countries people worship hundreds of gods carved from wood or stone. Why? Because they want to be "good," and they think this is the way.

Mothers have thrown their children to crocodiles as a sacrifice to their gods. The Bible mentions people causing their children to pass through fire as offerings to a god called Molech. Leviticus 18:21; 20:1-5.

In the National Museum at Mexico City sits a large, flat sacrificial stone where the ancient Indians laid the heads of human sacrifices for sin.

Some wash in rivers to get rid of their sins. Some make long journeys to "holy" places. Some wear burlap next to their skin, and the more it itches, the more merit they think they have gained.

All these ways and many others represent our futile efforts to save ourselves, to make ourselves righteous. We have an incurable bent to justify ourselves.

It all began with Adam. Adam attempted to solve his sin problem by wearing fig leaves. But God replaced the leaves with animal skins (Genesis 3:21), which required the death of the animals. This indicated that the real solution is death—the death of Jesus as man's Substitute. Genesis 3:15. Jesus chose death that we might have life.

Many people ask why Christians make such a big thing out of Jesus' death. "Haven't thousands of other men died on crosses?" they ask. The answer is Yes. Many people were crucified in ancient Rome, and many others have died for their country, friends, and family members. But Jesus' death was as high above all these as the heaven is high above the earth.

No one else died for every person. But Jesus did. He gave up His life for everyone. Hebrews 2:9; 2 Corinthians 5:14, 15. Nobody else could do it. Why? Because only Christ, as the Creator and God-man, could be the Substitute for the guilty race. Only He could have the sins of all laid upon Him. Only His death could pay the penalty for man's transgressions. No one else in all the universe was big enough to pay the whole cost.

By dying, Christ opened a way for us to be saved. His death makes it possible for us to be accepted of God. We can, through Him, receive forgiveness and a brand-new heart.

If Jesus is no more than a great teacher and a good man, His death would mean nothing to us. It would not secure our salvation any more than the others who died under imperial Rome.

The cross is the only way to heaven. There is no other road. Jesus says, "I am the way, the truth, and the life: no man cometh unto the Father, but by Me." John 14:6.

The cross reaches from the gate of Eden into all eternity. Abel accepted God's plan. He sacrificed a lamb to show his faith in the future death of Jesus. Abel's sins were forgiven, and God declared him righteous. Hebrews 11:4.

Cain rejected the Lord's way. He followed his own plan, but his offering of fruit was inadequate because it failed to point to Christ. The Bible says that "without the shedding of blood there is no forgiveness of sins." Hebrews 9:22, RSV. Cain's sins were not forgiven, for his offering did not show faith in the Lord's remedy.

Ever since Cain and Abel the issue has been accepting the Lord's solution for sin, or man's solutions. The Lord's way to righteousness is through faith in Christ. Man's way is by his own works, self-justification, auto-salvation.

Millions follow human philosophy to make themselves good. But human principles can never forgive our sins or change our heart. Some think they can make themselves right if their good deeds outweigh their bad deeds. Others think they can solve the problem by developing the good within them. Some attempt to do it by keeping the Ten Commandments.

Others try by self-discipline and self-improvement. All these things are good. But none of them can pardon our sins. None can give a new nature. None can change our destructive tendencies.

All our attempts at self-saving are inadequate. They never change our sinful hearts. Mark 7:21-23; Jeremiah 13:23; 17:9. They never free us from the dominion of sin. Pardon, righteousness, justification, and salvation are gifts from God. They are received only by faith in the Lord Jesus Christ.

There is no other way to solve our sin problem than by accepting Christ and His righteousness. "Neither is there salvation in any other: for there is none other name under heaven given among men, whereby we must be saved." Acts 4:12.

"Whosoever believeth in Him shall receive remission of sins." Acts 10:43. "Whosoever believeth in Him should not perish, but have eternal life." John 3:15.

God makes us right with Himself and keeps us right each day. This is justification by faith.

Man-made solutions just don't work.

God's Solution

Mr. Williams was a gardener. He kept the lawns and gardens of a rich man's estate. After several years Mr. Williams decided he would like to be self-employed. He quit working for the rich man and struck out on his own. Because he was an expert gardener, he had no trouble finding work. Everything went well until his wife developed a heart condition and two of his children were injured in a car accident. Debts piled up.

He borrowed a thousand dollars to meet some of his most pressing bills. But when it came time to pay back the loan, he simply did not have the money. And to make matters worse, a sudden attack of arthritis paralyzed him. He could not even earn a living.

The rich man for whom he had worked so many years went to the bank. He wrote a check for a thousand dollars and handed it in at the collection desk. "This cancels Mr. Williams's note," he said.

Then he went to the clerk. "Starting today my checking account is a joint account with Mr. Williams," he said. "Any checks he writes are to be charged to my account."

If you think Mr. Williams is lucky, you have not yet realized what God has done for you. You are not able to pay your sin debts. But when you receive Christ as your personal Saviour, God gives you credit for the perfect righteousness of Christ.

This cancels your past sins instantly. Romans 4:5-8. You then have a joint account with Christ. You can draw on His all-sufficient righteousness and saving power. He will enable you to live right each day.

When Christ was born, the angel said, "I have good news for you: there is great joy coming to the whole people." Luke 2:10, NEB. This good news was Christ—God's gift to save us from eternal death. He made His Son to be sin for you and me, that we, through Jesus, may be made the goodness of God. 2 Corinthians 5:21.

Christ became your Substitute. God, in Christ, was reconciling the world to Himself. 2 Corinthians 5:19. Christ "is Himself the remedy for the defilement of . . . the sins of all the world." 1 John 2:2, NEB.

The good news is that every person is pardoned, justified, and accepted through Christ. This gift is for you. It becomes yours the moment you receive Christ as your personal Saviour.

"All are justified by God's free grace alone, through His act of liberation in the person of Christ Jesus. For God designed Him to be the means of expiating sin by His sacrificial death, effective through faith. God meant by this to demonstrate His justice, because in His forbearance He had overlooked the sins of the past—to demonstrate His justice now in the present, showing that He is Himself just and also justifies any man who puts his faith in Jesus." Romans 3:24-26, NEB.

We are justified. We are declared righteous. God justifies any person who believes in Jesus. God loves each of us, has pardoned, justified, and accepted us in His Son.

"Oh that men would praise the Lord for His goodness, and for His wonderful works to the children of men." Psalm 107:8. "Be glad in the Lord, and rejoice, ye righteous: and shout for joy, all ye that are upright in heart." Psalm 32:11.

Do not hesitate, wondering, "Will God forgive me? Will He accept me?" God has already forgiven and justified you. Will you accept His forgiveness and justification?

You might think, "Since Christ died for all, and therefore God has pardoned and justified all, how can any be condemned by the Lord for his sins?" We can be condemned because we choose condemnation.

There is universal pardon and justification in Christ. But they cannot become yours until you accept Christ.

If you want light at night, you flick on the wall switch. If you do not do that you are in darkness, even though light is instantly available.

That's the way it is with pardon and salvation. They are available. But you must surrender to and believe in Christ. Then they become yours.

We are not condemned because we are born with a sinful nature. We are condemned because we will not accept Christ's sacrifice. If we know truth and do not obey it, then we are condemned. James 4:17. "He that believeth not is condemned already, because he hath not believed in the name of the only-begotten Son of God." John 3:18.

We all have problems. Some have more than others. It is impossible to live without encountering difficulties and trials. The Bible says, "Man is born unto trouble, as the sparks fly upward." Job 5:7.

But your most serious problem is sin. Examine yourself. Have you said and done things that hurt others? Have you ignored needs you could have met? Have you dwelt on impure or violent thoughts? We all have done these things. It's our nature.

We cannot change our heart. In Jeremiah 13:23 God asks, "Can the Ethiopian change his skin, or the leopard his spots?" We reply, "Of course not. That's how they are born." In the same way it is impossible for us to solve our sin problem. It is born with us.

We cannot change ourselves. But God can. Through His love He devised a way. That way is Christ. "For when we were yet without strength, in due time Christ died for the ungodly." Romans 5:6.

We have to eat to live. That is a law. Some years ago an official in Ireland refused to obey this law. He died in seventy-two days.

There was nothing arbitrary about the law or his death. He chose to disobey the natural law. That was his privilege. By choosing to disobey, he chose to die.

There are also spiritual laws. They are as real as physical laws. We choose: Obey and live. Disobey and perish. Accept and be saved. Reject and be lost.

All of God's commands are for our benefit. Deuteronomy 6:25. If we refuse God's solution we only hurt ourselves.

Man is a free moral agent. In the final analysis we choose heaven or hell. The best thing we can do is decide to follow Christ all the way. This is the most vital decision of life.

If we were wealthy, powerful, famous, and admired, but did not let God solve our sin problem, we would be in the worst possible position. It would be better for us if we had never been born. The glory and happiness of life could never really be ours.

Jesus said, "Ye will not come to Me, that ye might have life." John 5:40. The good news does us no good if we do not act on it. By our lack of faith we prevent Jesus from saving us.

No one can truthfully say, "I can't be saved." If you want to, you can be saved. If you do not want to, God will respect your decision. He will not arbitrarily force salvation on you if you do not want it.

But God sends the Holy Spirit to influence us to accept Christ. The Spirit urges us to accept God's free gift of eternal life. But it never, never forces. We decide. We choose.

"And the Spirit and the bride say, Come. And let him that heareth say, Come. And let him that is athirst come. And whosoever will, let him take the water of life freely." Revelation 22:17. Use your power of choice and say, "Jesus, I come."

Saved by Grace

The gas station owner filled out his weekly deposit slip. Fifteen hundred dollars in cash lay at his elbow.

"Help! Help me!" his mechanic yelled. He ran into the garage. A new jack was slowly collapsing. The mechanic lay under the car, trying to hold it up from crushing him. The station owner ran to the jack and pumped it up again.

While the owner was rescuing his mechanic, a man entered the main office to see him. This man had robbed the gas station of $1,000 six years before. Now he stood beside the cash and waited for the owner to return. He made no move to grab the money. He didn't even want to. Why? What made the difference? Three words: *Saved by grace.*

Grace means undeserved or unmerited favor. God favors us by solving our sin problem through Jesus. Christ was treated as we deserve to be treated. He accepted our punishment so we could be treated as He deserves. He exchanged places with us and became our Substitute.

God offers us justification and salvation as free gifts. You cannot earn them by good works or obedience. You receive them as gifts—free from Him to you.

"For by grace are ye saved through faith; and that not of yourselves: it is the gift of God: not of works, lest any man should boast." Ephesians 2:8, 9.

On a recent trip I bought a watch for my wife. When I got home, I held out the present. "Here," I said. "A little gift."

She had no part in making the watch. She did not pay for it. It was hers from the time I bought it. But it did not become actually hers until she accepted it. All she had to do was take it.

You can accept Christ's gift. Just reach out and take it. Faith "is the hand by which we lay hold upon Christ, and appropriate His merits, the remedy for sin."—Ellen G. White, *The Desire of Ages,* page 175. Reach out! Accept Christ's pardon, righteousness, salvation, and victory. They are yours.

Jesus died your death. He was your Substitute. That is the core of God's solution to sin. But there are also other features.

Christ, the God-man, lived a sinless life. He died, rose from the dead, and ascended into heaven. He was seated at the right hand of God the Father. He became man's Mediator and Advocate.

God did all this to give you freedom from sin and its penalty. How much did you do? Absolutely nothing. How much can you contribute or add to His labors? Not one ounce. This is why justification and salvation are not, and cannot be, partly by faith and partly by works. They are completely free, gifts from the unearned favor of God.

Justification is not earned by obeying the Ten Commandments or any other set of rules.

"We know that no man is ever justified by doing what the law demands, but only through faith in Christ Jesus." "When you seek to be justified by way of law, your relation with Christ is completely severed: you have fallen out of the domain of God's grace." Galatians 2:16; 5:4, NEB.

"Does this mean that we are using faith to undermine law? By no means: we are placing law itself on a firmer footing." Romans 3:31, NEB.

Instead of faith releasing us from obedience to the law, it enables us to obey. Romans 8:7, 3, 4. Through faith Christ's strength becomes our own.

Justification by faith places the law on a firmer footing.

If we follow the Bible truth, we will not try to save ourselves by obeying the law. But we also will not throw out the law.

The moment we are justified by faith, God gives us a new heart and pours His love into it. Romans 5:1-6. Then we have a love-filled faith. Paul said this kind of faith is the "only thing that counts." Galatians 5:6, NEB.

God's love in our heart produces a willing, happy obedience to His Ten Commandments. "Love means following the commandments of God." 2 John 6, NEB. Jesus said, "If you love Me, you will keep My commandments." John 14:15, RSV. He summed up the Ten in love to God and to our fellow human beings. Matthew 22:35-40.

We continually try to save ourselves. Many think they can earn salvation by obedience, good deeds, and missionary work. But the moment we think we earn salvation, we have lost it. A Christian is not saved because he is good, but he becomes good and does good because he is saved.

Justification and salvation are God's gifts. They are free, never earned partly by faith and partly by works. "If it is by grace, then it does not rest on deeds done, or grace would cease to be grace." "If without any work to his credit he simply puts his faith in Him who acquits the guilty, then his faith is indeed 'counted as righteousness.' " Romans 11:6; 4:5, NEB.

Good works and obedience are essential after a person is justified. But they are the natural result of a genuine loving faith. They are the outgrowth of God's love in the heart. They express openly what God has done in the life. But they are never the way to salvation.

Repentance has an essential place in God's solution of our sin problem. Paul summed up the way of salvation as "repentance toward God, and faith toward our Lord Jesus Christ." Acts 20:21. Repentance and faith in Jesus are two facets of God's plan for salvation.

Saving faith leads us to do right, when before we did wrong. We obey the Ten Commandments instead of transgressing them. John 14:21-24; 1 John 5:3. Saving faith includes repentance, confession, conversion, obedience, baptism, and a daily consecration to God. When Christ lives in us thus, complete faith is ours.

Never before were there so many professed Christians yet so little genuine New Testament Christianity. This is because many of us disregard the essential features of faith in Christ.

2 Timothy 3:1-5 lists eighteen sins practiced by those who have only a form of godliness, but no Saviour in their heart. Their faith in Christ is inadequate and deficient.

Financial, social, racial, and educational advantages mean nothing to God. Justification by faith lays man's boasting in the dust. It accomplishes for him what he cannot do for himself.

It is up to us to kneel at the foot of the cross. Surrender self to Christ. Then receive pardon and peace, justification and salvation, by faith in Christ. There is no other way. There can be no other way.

"God forbid that I should glory, save in the cross of our Lord Jesus Christ, by whom the world is crucified unto me, and I unto the world." Galatians 6:14.

All the credit belongs to Christ. He is the only one who can save us.

The redeemed will sing, "Worthy is the Lamb that was slain to receive . . . honor, and glory, and blessing." "Thou art worthy . . . : for Thou wast slain, and hast redeemed us to God by Thy blood." Revelation 5:12, 9.

Only Believe

Could two prisoners, singing a duet, cause an earthquake to shake open the prison doors and set them free? This is what happened in the prison at Philippi when Paul and Silas sang at midnight. Acts 16:22-28.

The jailer asked, "What must I do to be saved?" He wanted to solve his sin problem. Paul and Silas answered, "Believe on the Lord Jesus Christ, and thou shalt be saved." Acts 16:30, 31.

Because of this and certain other verses, some think that all we need to do for salvation is to believe in Christ. This is true, if we believe the way the Bible stipulates.

Those who insist that all we have to do is to believe in Christ, seldom realize what the Bible means by "believing in Christ." Believing in Christ is not merely a mental assent that He is the Son of God and the only Saviour. If we go no farther than this, we do not have salvation. Even the devils have this kind of belief. James 2:19; Luke 4:41.

Accepting Christ is not just saying, "I am a Jesus person. I am on my way to heaven."

The greatest deception of the human mind is that a mere assent to truth constitutes righteousness. While we need the intellectual conviction for Christ, we also need to receive Him into our heart. "For with the heart man believeth unto righteousness." Romans 10:10.

"Believe on the Lord Jesus Christ" was only the first part of Paul's answer to the jailer's question. The next verse says, "They spake unto him the word of the Lord, and to all that were in his house." Acts 16:30-32. Paul and Silas explained what was involved in believing on Jesus. This essential procedure is often left undone today.

"As many as received Him [Christ], to them gave He power to become the sons of God, *even to them that believe on His name: which were born, not of blood, . . . but of God.*" John 1:12, 13.

To believe on Jesus for salvation is to receive Him into our hearts and lives, to be regenerated into new persons. Jesus Christ, in response to our faith, enters into us as our personal Saviour.

When the electric current enters a light at night, the darkness vanishes. And when Christ enters a person, sin vanishes. Christ re-creates him spiritually into a new person. He lives a new life, even the life of Christ. "Therefore, if anyone is in Christ, he is a new creation; the old has passed away, behold, the new has come." 2 Corinthians 5:17, RSV.

When we truly believe on Christ, we are made into a new person. The former sins drop off, and Christ lives His life of righteousness in us.

Real believing on Jesus involves a laying "aside that old human nature, which, deluded by its lusts, is sinking toward death" and a putting on "the new nature of God's creating, which shows itself in the just and devout life called for by the truth." Ephesians 4:22-24, NEB. This is a choice we must make.

This is real conversion. This is being born of God. "Except a man be born again, he cannot see the kingdom of God." John 3:3. "The only thing that counts is new creation." Galatians 6:16, NEB. No one has truly believed on Jesus until this miraculous change takes place in him.

The one way to solve your sin problem is by the renewing and transforming grace of Jesus operating within. This begins with conversion. And then comes a constant advancement as Christ lives in you.

Real faith in the Son of God means that Christ lives in you.

When a believer has Christ living in him, Jesus brings him into harmony with God's requirements. The Bible emphasizes the inseparable connection between obedience to God's commandments and true belief in Christ. "Here is the test by which we can make sure that we know Him: do we keep His commands? The man who says, 'I know Him,' while he disobeys His commands, is a liar and a stranger to the truth; but in the man who is obedient to His word, the divine love has indeed come to its perfection." 1 John 2:3-5, NEB.

True faith always obeys God. "If it does not lead to action, it is in itself a lifeless thing." James 2:17, NEB.

The Bible gives many examples of people who had true faith. In every case they did exactly what God asked them to do. Faith in Jesus and obedience are inseparable.

Jesus said it is useless to call Him Lord if we do not obey Him. "And why call ye Me, Lord, Lord, and do not the things which I say?" Luke 6:46.

Is Christ living His life in you, giving you the ability to obey God?

Many reduce believing on Jesus to an ecstatic feeling. True Christian experience is always based on faith, not on feeling. "The just shall live by faith." Romans 1:17.

Countless thousands say, "I believe that Christ died for my sins." This is an essential step. But unless our will is fully surrendered to Christ, our belief in Christ is useless.

Some may say, "I go to church regularly; I read my Bible and pray daily; I try to live a good life." But unless our belief in Christ leads to the full surrender of our will to Him, it fails. "So likewise, whosoever he be of you that forsaketh not all that he hath, he cannot be My disciple." Luke 14:33.

Jesus said, "Abide in Me, and I in you." Faith is dwelling in Christ, and Christ dwelling in us. He said, "If a man abide not in Me, he is cast forth as a branch, and is withered; and men gather them, and cast them into the fire, and they are burned." John 15:4, 6.

"I am crucified with Christ: nevertheless I live; yet not I, but

Christ liveth in me: and the life which I now live in the flesh I live by the faith of the Son of God, who loved me, and gave Himself for me." Galatians 2:20.

Paul lived every day through faith in Christ. What did this mean? He answers: "I am crucified with Christ: . . . Christ liveth in me." True believing on Jesus is a daily rejection of sin and the living of Christ within the believer. This kind of believing on Christ is all that you need to be saved.

Freedom from sin involves a constant attitude of believing in Jesus. It requires daily surrender, a constant yielding of the heart and life to Christ.

The person believing on Him who continues to believe and who makes it a life habit is being saved. John 3:18, 36. Let us make sure that we have this belief in Jesus.

Achieving Through Believing

Everything connected with becoming and remaining a Christian is a part of believing on Jesus. Faith includes repentance, confession, restitution, pardon, justification, the new birth, baptism, obedience to Christ's commandments, the indwelling of the Holy Spirit, daily feeding on the Word, prayer, Christian growth, worshiping, and witnessing.

The initial experience is believing on Christ and receiving Him into the heart. Then comes the daily belief in Christ, so that Christ lives His life in us. These two phases of believing go together.

On the Day of Pentecost many cried out, "Men and brethren, what shall we do?" Peter told them: "Repent, and be baptized every one of you in the name of Jesus Christ for the remission of sins, and ye shall receive the gift of the Holy Ghost." Acts 2:37, 38.

Peter mentioned four particular items: repentance, pardon, baptism, and the gift of the Holy Spirit.

These four are not all the essential features of believing on Jesus. "And *with many other words* did he testify and exhort." Acts 2:40. True repentance includes a turning away from sin. It brings obedience to God. It leads into full surrender, conversion, and daily consecration. If a believer does not reject his former sins, he does not believe on Christ. "Let everyone that nameth the name of Christ depart from iniquity." 2 Timothy 2:19.

Conversions vary with each person. Some are instantaneous. Others are gradual over a period of time. But in every case there comes a climactic moment when the person is born again and passes from death to life.

Repentance, confession, pardon, and conversion are continuing aspects of the Christian life.

Daily consecration is necessary after we receive Christ. Paul spoke of being renewed day by day. 2 Corinthians 4:16. The lack of this new conversion each day is why so many believers don't have a dynamic, growing experience.

The Holy Spirit is our greatest and most essential gift from God. We depend completely upon Him. The Holy Spirit alone produces true conviction and repentance. He alone draws to Christ. He alone regenerates us, purifies our heart, and gives us power to overcome sin. He grants us the continual presence of Christ. He brings Christ into our hearts. We live the Christian life each day through the power of the Holy Spirit.

Paul says that the Spirit of God dwelling in you is Christ in you. "You are on the spiritual level, if only God's Spirit dwells within you; and if a man does not possess the Spirit of Christ [the Holy Spirit] , he is no Christian." Romans 8:9, 10, NEB.

Jesus taught that the Holy Spirit living within is Christ in the Christian. John 14:16-18, 20, 23. Christ revealed the secret of His incomparable life: "I am in the Father, and the Father in Me." John 14:10. Then He showed that the secret of right living is for us to be in Christ and Christ in us through the Holy Spirit.

The only way any person can live a true Christian life is to let Christ live in him moment by moment. This is the secret of a happy, victorious Christian experience. *The secret is this: Christ in you,* the hope of a glory to come." Colossians 1:27, NEB.

When Jesus was here among men, He did not impose Himself upon those who felt self-sufficient, self-righteous. He did not force His way into hearts. But He never refused to help a person who needed and wanted Him. "As many as touched Him were made whole." Mark 6:56. Receive Him and be complete. Colossians 2:10.

His promise is, "Ye shall . . . find Me, when ye shall search for Me with all your heart." Jeremiah 29:13. Will you open the door of your life and let Him come in and complete you?

Christ says, "I stand at the door, and knock: if any man hear My voice, and open the door, I will come in to him, and will sup with him, and he with Me." Revelation 3:20. This promise of Christ is to you. Put your own name into His promise, instead of "any man" and "him." Assert your faith. God will honor it.

When someone knocks at our door, or rings the doorbell, we know he wants to come in. Jesus knocks at the door of our lives. The Holy Spirit gives us thoughts and desires for God. If you have not already given Him full control of your life, will you open the door now?

Open your door by fully surrendering to Him. Surrender your intellect, will, and total personality. Then believe that Christ comes into your life to forgive all your sins and set you free.

The door which admits Jesus opens only from the inside. It is by your own decision that He can enter in.

Bow your head just now and pray: "Lord Jesus, I need You more than anything else. I receive You as my Saviour. I surrender all to You. I now open the door of my life. And I thank You that according to Your promise, You are in me and have forgiven all my sins. Live in me continually. I ask it all in Your name. Amen."

Jesus never fails to fulfill His promise when we meet the conditions. Admit your need. Commit yourself to Him. Permit Him to live and work in you. Transmit His love to others.

In faith you can say, "I have Jesus according to His unfailing promise, and He has me. All my sins have been forgiven. He will live His life in me."

"He that believeth on the Son of God hath the witness in himself." 1 John 5:10. Every person who exercises true faith in Christ finds the solution to his sin problem.

Only your faith limits God's possibilities. "If thou canst believe, all things are possible to him that believeth." Mark 9:23. Jesus says, "Ask, and ye shall receive, that your joy may be full." John 16:24.

You Are Accepted

As a woman wrote a letter, a drop of ink accidentally fell on her white silk handkerchief. This kerchief, a gift from a very dear friend, was important to her. Now it was ruined. She felt miserable.

Shortly after this, while attending a social gathering, she met John Ruskin, the famous art critic and writer. She mentioned how she had ruined her most prized handkerchief. "Let me take it home," Ruskin said, "and see what I can do with it."

He drew a lovely picture on the kerchief, working the ink blot into the drawing. When he was finished, the kerchief looked as though it had never been spoiled.

She valued it more highly than when it was new because it now revealed a drawing by a great man.

The image of God in man has been marred by sin. But the Master Artist offers to restore this image. When we receive Him, He covers the sin blots with His righteousness. Then we stand faultless before God. We are not condemned when we are in Christ Jesus. Romans 8:1. If we continue cooperating with Christ, God's image will be fully restored in us.

A man applies for a desirable job. He receives a letter saying that he has been accepted for it. He is happy. He doesn't say, "I hope I will be accepted for this job." He knows that he has been accepted. It is written in the letter. When you receive Christ, and believe what God has written, you can know that He accepts you.

If you give yourself to Christ and accept Him as your Saviour, you are accounted righteous. Christ stands in the place of your sinful character. God accepts you just as if you had not sinned.

Christ's character fills in the place of your character; His goodness replaces your sins.

Repeat this, and let it sink deep into your heart and mind: "I now give myself to Christ and receive Him as my personal Saviour. In spite of my past sins, I am accounted righteous. Christ's character replaces mine. God accepts me just as if I had not sinned." You are not only forgiven, but God treats you as a perfect being in Christ. In Christ you are just as if you'd never sinned. Justification by faith is as sweet as honey, as refreshing as a spring of cold water in a hot desert.

Many earnest people who come to Christ doubt that He accepts them. But there need be no uncertainty *if you act* upon what God has said.

The good news is that "*He hath made us accepted* in the Beloved." Ephesians 1:6. When you receive Christ there is no question as to whether or not God will accept you. You have been accepted. Will you take the gift of life from Christ's pierced hand and enjoy it?

If doubts trouble you, surrender fully to Christ. Repeat five times the personal acceptance mentioned above. Believe it as you say it.

God accepts you as you are if you are willing to obey Him. "For if there be first a willing mind, it is accepted according to that a man hath, and not according to that he hath not." 2 Corinthians 8:12. If anyone believes in Christ, he is not rejected because of what he lacks.

It is God's purpose that every person who accepts and obeys Christ receive eternal life. Jesus said, "And this is the will of Him that sent Me, that everyone which seeth the Son, and believeth on Him, may have everlasting life: and I will raise him up at the last day." John 6:40.

God's promises are always true. When your faith takes hold of His eternal purpose, your acceptance is as sure as He is.

The Bible is the Book of hope for each of us.

"Him that cometh to Me I will in no wise cast out." John 6:37.

Be certain that Christ receives, forgives, justifies, cleanses, and accepts you, for He does—through your faith.

The Lord has no favorites. "Thus saith the Lord that created thee, . . . Fear not: for I have redeemed thee, I have called thee by thy name; thou art Mine." Isaiah 43:1.

Do not say, "I hope Jesus will redeem me." He says, "I have redeemed thee." He calls you by your name. ".............., come unto Me and enjoy pardon, justification, salvation, and victory." Don't hesitate! Come.

Do not rob yourself of the joy and peace of full forgiveness for your sins. Assert your faith in His promise. He says, "I have blotted out, as a thick cloud, thy transgressions . . . : return unto Me: for I *have* redeemed thee." Isaiah 44:22.

When you receive Christ, your sins *have been* blotted out. They are covered with Christ's righteousness.

"Sing, O ye heavens; for the Lord hath done it: shout, ye lower parts of the earth: break forth into singing, ye mountains, O forest, and every tree therein: for the Lord hath redeemed Jacob, and glorified Himself in Israel." Isaiah 44:23.

"Every soul may say: 'By His perfect obedience He has satisfied the claims of the law, and my only hope is found in looking to Him as my substitute and surety, who obeyed the law perfectly for me. By faith in His merits I am free from the condemnation of the law. He clothes me with His righteousness, which answers all the demands of the law. I am complete in Him who brings in everlasting righteousness. He presents me to God in the spotless garment of which no thread was woven by any human agent. All is of Christ, and all the glory, honor and majesty are to be given to the Lamb of God, which taketh away the sins of the world.' "—Ellen G. White, *Selected Messages,* Bk. 1, p. 396.

GIVE YOUR GUILT AWAY

The gap between your lack and what you can have in Christ is bridged by your belief in the promises of God. Every failure or lack on our part is because of our weak faith.

You may receive a certified check made out to you for $1,000. But it will not help you until you endorse it and cash it. Through Christ, the promises of God are Yes for you. 2 Corinthians 1:20. Christ is God's certified check for your pardon, justification, acceptance, and salvation. Faith in Him is the needed endorsement. Through faith these priceless gifts are yours.

We settle for a few crumbs—and we could have a whole feast. "My God shall supply all your need." Philippians 4:19.

Righting Wrong

The soda fountain clerks went on strike in a certain city. One drugstore hired nonunion clerks. It did a tremendous business. There was scarcely standing room at the counter.

A union picket decided to sneak into the store and drop a stench bomb. This kind of bomb does not hurt people; it just oozes with a black liquid that smells so bad it drives everyone out of the room.

The store manager had prepared for this kind of trouble. He watched the entrance carefully. He saw the man enter and noticed the bulge under his coat. He confronted the man just as the stench bomb dropped. Immediately the manager poured a white powder on the black liquid.

This powder changed the stench into a fresh, sweet odor. The customers in the store didn't know what had happened, but they were delighted by the freshness that filled the room.

Likewise the Lord by His love and grace gives us the perfect righteousness of Christ. Then we change from guilt to innocence, from being sinful to being righteous in God's sight. This is justification by faith.

God's way of righting wrong is through faith in Christ. All who have such faith receive God's pardon. Romans 2:22.

It is not enough for family, friends, or neighbors to think we are "good." We must be righteous in the sight of God. Nothing less than perfect goodness can make us right in the sight of God. We cannot reach such a goal by all our good works or obedience, only by receiving Christ's righteousness by faith.

The goodness of God is embodied in Christ. We receive this goodness when we receive Him. We have it continually while we keep Christ. And we are the righteousness of God through Him. 2 Corinthians 5:21.

Christians who have received Christ's goodness are declared to be "the incense offered by Christ to God." 2 Corinthians 2:15, NEB. The righteousness of Christ makes us acceptable and pleasing to God.

"The only way in which he can attain to righteousness is through faith. By faith he can bring to God the merits of Christ, and the Lord places the obedience of His Son to the sinner's account. Christ's righteousness is accepted in place of man's failure, and God *receives, pardons, justifies, the repentant, believing soul,* treats him as though he were righteous, and loves him as He loves His Son. *This is how faith is accounted righteousness;* and the pardoned soul goes on from grace to grace, from light to greater light."—Ellen G. White, *Selected Messages,* Bk. 1, p. 367. (Emphasis supplied.)

The only way our sin problem can be solved is for Christ to give us His goodness. This is why "our only ground of hope is in the righteousness of Christ imputed to us, and in that wrought by His Spirit working in and through us."—Ellen G. White, *Steps to Christ,* page 63.

The Word says, "God imputeth righteousness without works." Romans 4:6. "Impute" means to credit to someone's account—to attribute something to someone else.

When you receive Jesus as your Saviour, God gives you credit for the perfect goodness of Christ. His goodness covers all your past sins. You stand before God just as if you had not sinned. Christ takes your sins and gives you His righteousness. No wonder Martin Luther exclaimed, "With what love He [Christ] opens His arms to you, taking all your sins upon Himself and giving you all His righteousness."

His imputed righteousness provides for a complete exchange. Christ's goodness replaces our guilt, our failures, our sins. How grateful and happy we should be that when we receive Christ, His perfect goodness stands in the place of our sins and failures.

"By the obedience of One shall many be made righteous." Romans 5:19.

This crediting of Christ's righteousness wipes out our past sins. But we are immediately confronted with another aspect of our sin problem. How can we live righteously for the remainder of our life? How can we be kept from sin each day?

At the same time that Christ's goodness gives pardon for our past sins, the Holy Spirit creates a new heart in us. We are then born of God by the Spirit. Christ makes His home in us through the Holy Spirit. And by living His life in us, Christ imparts His goodness to us moment by moment. This is how we are kept from sin each day.

"Impart" means to share with another, to give to someone else. Christ's goodness is His life. When He lives His life in us, His goodness becomes ours.

"Christ liveth in me." Galatians 2:20. This is imparted righteousness. This is sanctification.

Righteousness by faith is God's solution for your sin problem. Imputed plus imparted righteousness equals salvation. Receiving Christ plus letting Him live within you equals the solution to your sin problem.

After we are justified, we must continually receive Christ's goodness to move forward.

It takes this goodness of Christ within us to keep us from sin. There is no way we can do right until our heart is made right. And we can be kept right only as Christ lives in us. We must have Christ's righteousness credited to us and given to us. These are actually inseparable. We receive and have both when we receive and retain Christ.

Christ's goodness clothes us. This is the only way God can accept us.

Imputed righteousness pardons our past sins. We are justified by faith. Imparted righteousness regenerates us into a new person. Christ lives in our renewed heart. Imputed and imparted righteousness constitute the robe of Christ's goodness. God never condemns us when we wear Christ's righteousness. Romans 8:1.

Even when we do our best to obey God, we still make mistakes and have deficiencies. Christ's given goodness makes up for these so that we may be perfect in Him every day. Colossians 1:28.

"When it is in the heart to obey God, when efforts are put forth to this end, Jesus accepts this disposition and effort as man's best service, and He makes up for the deficiency with His own divine merit."—Ellen G. White, *Selected Messages,* Bk. 1, p. 382.

The little green apple has a relative perfection. But it needs to grow, to mature. If it does not grow and develop, it loses its relative perfection.

That is how it is when we receive Christ. He clothes us in the robe of His perfect righteousness. He lives in us by faith. We are perfect in Him every day. And there will be continual advancement "unto the measure of the stature of the fullness of Christ." Ephesians 4:13. There will be a continuing transformation as the character of Christ is reproduced in us. Romans 12:2; 2 Corinthians 3:18.

This is how we grow. Go to God in prayer each day. Read His Word. Obey Him moment by moment. Witness for Christ through your life and words.

The Priceless Free Robe

A king held an elaborate wedding banquet to celebrate the marriage of his son. Many were invited. With each invitation a wedding garment was provided. One guest thought his own suit was better than the wedding garment.

When he appeared at the wedding without the garment, he was bound hand and foot by the king's servants and thrown out into the darkness.

The wedding garment represents the robe of Christ's goodness. This priceless robe is free. None are prepared to enter heaven unless they wear the robe of His righteousness.

This is confirmed in the book of Revelation. In a vision John saw many people from all nations gathered before God's throne in heaven after the second coming of Christ. The angel identified these as people who "have washed their robes, and made them white in the blood of the Lamb." Revelation 7:14.

Washing our robes is being made perfect through Christ's righteousness. The Bible identifies justification by His blood with being justified by His righteousness. Romans 5:9; 3:25, 26.

All who are gathered to heaven will wear these white robes, because they were all saved by the free gift of Christ's righteousness. They will not need His righteousness in heaven for the pardon of sin or for being saved from sin. But the robe will testify to their complete dependence upon Christ for salvation.

35

They will sing a hymn of praise to the Lamb. Why? "For Thou wast slain, and hast redeemed us to God by Thy blood." Revelation 5:9.

Why did the man who was thrown out of the wedding feast try to attend without the provided wedding garment? Obviously he preferred his own clothes. Self-righteousness prevents many professed Christians from having the goodness of Christ. Allowing one's self-righteousness to keep him from being clothed in the robe of Christ's righteousness is fatal.

In the time of Christ, God's own people had lapsed into legalism and a sterile formalism. They ignored God's goodness and were bent on establishing their own righteousness. Romans 10:3; 9:31-33. They were so self-deceived that they sincerely believed they had God's righteousness, even when they were plotting to kill Jesus.

Self-righteousness claims, "I am rich, and increased with goods, and have need of nothing." When a person has his own righteousness instead of Christ's righteousness, he is "wretched, and miserable, and poor, and blind, and naked," and knows it not. Revelation 3:17. Paul, before he received Christ, thought he had God's righteousness when he was torturing or killing Christians. That's how deceived his self-estimate was.

Self-righteousness is always a trap. We think we are right when we are wrong. The consequences are fatal.

Self-righteousness results in self-pleasing, self-glorification, self-praise, self-seeking, self-satisfaction, self-serving, self-sufficiency, self-conceit, self-deception, self-exaltation, self-indulgence, and self-justification. These traits exclude Christ from the heart. They keep us from receiving the goodness of Christ.

Christ's righteousness results in "love, joy, peace, patience, kindness, goodness, faithfulness, gentleness, self-control." Galatians 5:22, 23, RSV. This is life at its best.

If we do not have Christ's goodness, we will follow some form of self-righteousness. The basic issue of life involves a choice—self, or Christ. Self-righteousness, or Christ's righteousness. Jesus struck at the very heart of the issue when He said, "If anyone wishes to be a follower of Mine, he must leave self behind; day after day he must take up his cross, and come with Me." Luke 9:23, NEB.

Jesus warned against the danger of spiritual degeneration. "He saw that the weakness . . . would be a spirit of self-righteousness. Men would think they could do something toward earning a place in the kingdom of heaven. They would imagine that when they had made certain advancement, the Lord would come in to help them. Thus there would be an abundance of self and little of Jesus. Many who had made a little advancement would be puffed up and think themselves superior to others. They would be eager for flattery, jealous if not thought most important. Against this danger Christ seeks to guard His disciples."—Ellen G. White, *Christ's Object Lessons,* pages 400, 401.

It is impossible for a person to have Christ's righteousness when he relies on his own righteousness. A person must reject his own selfishness before he can receive Christ's goodness. There must be a daily crucifixion of self so that Jesus can live in us.

Christ said of the Pharisees, "Their worship of Me is in vain, for they teach as doctrines the commandments of men." Matthew 15:9, NEB. Any substituting of man's thoughts for the commandments and teachings of God is a form of righteousness by works. Millions of people have a mixture of truth and error.

Think of a few of these man-made substitutes: A social gospel instead of Christ's spiritual gospel. Self-realization instead of divine regeneration. Self-improvement instead of true conversion. Positive thinking instead of a new mind from the Holy Spirit. Situation ethics instead of God's law. A new Ten Commandments minus number four. A man-made, first-day, or Sunday sabbath instead of Christ's true seventh-day Sabbath. Sprinkling for baptism instead of immersion.

The Christian's title to heaven depends on his justification by Christ. At the same time, day by day, he is being fitted for heaven by sanctification—by being made holy.

Christ lives in the believer to save him from sin. But what if a Christian fails to give Christ full and continual control and falls into some sin? The only remedy is to repent. Confess it to God. Ask God to forgive you. "If we confess our sins, He is faithful and just to forgive us our sins." 1 John 1:9.

God never fails to fulfill His promises. He forgives as surely as you repent and confess. The imputed righteousness of Christ, which blotted out your sins when you came to Christ, still erases confessed sins afterward. 1 John 2:1, 2.

We wear the robe of Christ's righteousness only when Christ is in us every day. Jesus said, "Abide in Me, and I in you." John 15:4. This involves a daily consecration to God—a morning-by-morning opening of the door to Christ, the daily rejection of self, a continual obedience to the Lord's commandments. We cannot wear this robe without maintaining a living connection with Jesus. Then our desires are merged with Christ's. Our mind becomes one with Christ.

If we do not reject our sins, Christ cannot dwell in us. Faith is Forsaking-All-I-Take-Him. The goodness of Christ transforms us into His image.

Do you obey God because you have to, or because you want to? The answer may reveal whether you have on the robe of Christ's righteousness. When He lives in your heart, you will say, "I delight to do Thy will, O my God: yea, Thy law is within my heart." Psalm 40:8.

A person who thinks he is reasonably good will not hunger and thirst for Christ's righteousness. And he won't have it. Jesus said: "Blessed are they which do hunger and thirst after righteousness: for they shall be filled." Matthew 5:6.

Paul stated that he was determined to "be found in Him, not having mine own righteousness, which is of the law, but that which is through the faith of Christ, the righteousness which is of God by faith: that I may know Him, and the power of His resurrection, and the fellowship of His sufferings, being made conformable unto His death; if by any means I might attain unto the resurrection of the dead." Philippians 3:9-11.

Having Christ's righteousness is knowing Christ and experiencing His power.

"I am crucified with Christ: nevertheless I live; yet not I, but Christ liveth in me." Galatians 2:20.

"When He shall come with trumpet sound,
O may I then in Him be found;
Clad in His righteousness alone;
Faultless to stand before the throne."

Rags to Riches

You have heard stories of remarkable financial success. Some people begin with nothing and make themselves millionaires.

Spiritually we start with rags, filthy rags. "But we are all as an unclean thing, and all our righteousnesses are as filthy rags; and we all do fade as a leaf; and our iniquities, like the wind, have taken us away." Isaiah 64:6.

This verse tells it as it is. Our best efforts to save ourselves apart from Christ are as good as filthy rags.

But our filthy garments can be exchanged for the spotless robe of Christ's righteousness. And it's free!

Then the Lord said, "Take away the filthy garments. . . . Behold, I have caused thine iniquity to pass from thee, and I will clothe thee with change of raiment." Zechariah 3:4.

So it is when we receive Christ. Our sins are taken away. Our rags are exchanged for the spotless robe of Christ's righteousness. This is what Christ wants to do for you.

Why should you refuse God's offer of new clothes?

Picture it for yourself. Here you stand. Your only clothes are threadbare, ragged, and soiled. And someone offers you new clothes of the finest material, tailored to your size. He says, "I will be happy to give you these fine new clothes for the ones you have." How quickly you would accept that offer! Why not be as eager to accept Christ's spotless robe of righteousness in exchange for your sins?

Christ's goodness is available to all who will accept it. "None are so sinful that they cannot find strength, purity, and righteousness in Jesus, who died for them. He is waiting to strip them of their garments stained and polluted with sin, and to put upon them the white robes of righteousness."—Ellen G. White, *Steps to Christ,* page 53.

When we accept Christ, God does not see our sins, defects, failures, and faults. He sees the perfect life of His own Son in us. Such an offer! Christ's perfect righteousness in exchange for your sins.

Jesus was made sin for us so that we could be the righteousness of God in Him. 2 Corinthians 5:21. You have His righteousness in exchange for your sins.

This matter of being clothed in the robe of Christ's goodness should be a source of extraordinary joy. Isaiah said, "I will greatly rejoice in the Lord, my soul shall be joyful in my God; for . . . He hath covered me with the robe of righteousness." Isaiah 61:10.

Believers are not one half as happy as they should be. "May the God of hope fill you with all joy and peace by your faith in Him, until, by the power of the Holy Spirit, you overflow with hope." Romans 15:13, NEB.

Righteousness by faith is the richest gift given to us. A free gift. With it we can enter Christ's kingdom of heaven.

"For the promise, that he should be the heir of the world, was not to Abraham, or to his seed, through the law, but *through the righteousness of faith."* Romans 4:13.

God promised Abraham that he and his descendants would inherit the entire world. This promise refers to the new earth, which God will reconstruct after sin has been eradicated. Hebrews 11:8-10; 2 Peter 3:13.

An eternal inheritance in the perfect new earth does not depend upon our being literal descendants from Abraham. It depends on Christ's righteousness becoming ours through faith.

"In Christ indeed we *have been given our share in the heritage."* Ephesians 1:11, NEB. And what a heritage it is! Pardon

41

for all our sins. His righteousness upon us and in us. Justification. A new heart. Born again into a new person. Christ in our heart to live His life in us. His peace and His joy. Jesus as our dearest friend. The gift of the Holy Spirit. Eternal life. Everlasting happiness in heaven.

These are priceless. With this kind of inheritance you are a billionaire in Christ. "You have come into your fortune already." 1 Corinthians 4:8, NEB.

Christ's goodness accepted by faith day after day, transforms us into the likeness of Jesus. This is the essential preparation for having our body made like Christ's glorious body at His second coming. Philippians 3:20, 21.

Then we will have a perfect, immortal, incorruptible body like Christ's. No more sickness. No pain. No trouble. No sorrow. No old age. No death. Everlasting joy. Then the greatest space trip ever taken, and a mansion in the New Jerusalem. It is truly from rags to infinite riches when you exchange self-righteousness for Christ's goodness.

Through righteousness by faith the believer enters into "the unsearchable riches of Christ." Ephesians 3:8. He shares in the riches of His grace (Ephesians 1:7), the riches of His glory (Ephesians 3:8), the riches of God's goodness, forbearance, and long-suffering (Romans 2:4), the riches of the knowledge of God's truth (Romans 11:33), the riches of full assurance of understanding (Colossians 2:2). These are the true riches.

In the end the wealth of all the millionaires will sink into insignificance in contrast to these riches of righteousness by faith. The richest man in the world is poor if he does not have righteousness by faith. Enjoy your fortune in Christ.

Happiness Is Yours

An old blind man struggled to crawl up hundreds of steps leading to the top of a "sacred" mountain. If he could only reach the top, he thought, he would have gained sufficient merit to save himself. He was tired, frustrated, unhappy.

A tourist asked him, "What are you looking for?" "Oh," he said, "I'm searching for heaven and God." "Have you found Him?" asked the tourist. "No," replied the old man; "I feel and I feel, but somehow I cannot find the door."

How happy he might have been if he could have heard Jesus say, "Son, be of good cheer; thy sins be forgiven thee." Matthew 9:2. In the Lord Jesus Christ we have an open door to all that we need. Jesus said, "I am the door: by Me if any man enter in, he shall be saved." John 10:9.

Jesus loves you. He delights to forgive sins. He pardons freely and completely. He casts your sins behind His back. He sinks them in the depths of the sea.

God, in His amazing grace, is infinitely more ready and pleased to pardon than to condemn. "He hath not dealt with us after our sins; nor rewarded us according to our iniquities." Psalm 103:10.

Many Christians believe that the Old Testament teaches we can be righteous by keeping the Ten Commandments. They claim that Christians should follow only what is written in the New Testament, which teaches righteousness by faith in Jesus Christ.

Then they draw the conclusion that the commandments don't apply to Christians today.

But the entire Bible from Genesis to Revelation is one harmonious, progressive unfolding of the theme of righteousness by faith. The sacrificial system of the Old Testament was based on and pointed to the vicarious death of Christ. The dripping blood on Jewish altars proclaimed salvation only by grace.

When Adam sinned, he was justified by faith in Jesus Christ. There is no other way to be justified. "By the deeds of the law there shall no flesh be justified in His [God's] sight: for by the law is the knowledge of sin." Romans 3:20. The law proves that we are guilty of sin. It cannot justify. It condemns.

If we could be righteous by keeping the Ten Commandments, or any other rules, we would be our own savior. And Christ would not have had to die. It is written: "I do not nullify the grace of God; for if justification were through the law, then Christ died to no purpose." Galatians 2:21, RSV.

If the Ten Commandments could have been repealed, or set aside, Christ would not have had to die for our sins. Therefore Christ's crucifixion did not and could not annul the law.

When Christ lived on this earth He obeyed the Ten Commandments. He never changes. So when Christ lives His life in the true Christian there will be obedience to God's commandments.

Instead of canceling out the Ten Commandments, salvation by grace is God's way of enabling us to meet the law's requirements. Through Christ we obey every command of His.

"For what the law could not do, in that it was weak through the flesh, God sending His own Son in the likeness of sinful flesh, and for sin, condemned sin in the flesh: that the righteousness of the law might be fulfilled in us, who walk not after the flesh, but after the Spirit." Romans 8:3, 4. "Blessed are they whose iniquities are forgiven, and whose sins are covered. Blessed is the man to whom the Lord will not impute sin." Romans 4:7, 8.

Guilt is poison. People have been driven to suicide by it. Minds and bodies are injured by it. Christ alone can heal it. "With His stripes we are healed." Isaiah 53:5.

The guilt of sin makes us miserable. Full and free forgiveness from Christ makes us happy.

Then the Lord covers us with Christ's righteousness. God sees us as we are in Christ—clothed in the robe of His goodness.

"In those days, and in that time, saith the Lord, the iniquity of Israel shall be sought for, and there shall be none; and the sins of Judah, and they shall not be found: for I will pardon them whom I reserve." Jeremiah 50:20.

The lives of the Israelites were filled with sins and failures. But God covered the sins of those who accepted Christ by faith. Their sins were sought for, and could not be found. They stood before God as if they had never sinned. God forgives and then forgets our sins. Isaiah 43:25.

Some say, "If I could only live my life over again, I wouldn't have formed certain bad habits. I would have avoided them." But no one can do this. We can't change our past.

Christ offers us a new life, a new future. He can convert us and help us start over again. He blots out our past sins. He covers them with His righteousness. His perfect obedience stands in place of our sins. "The merits of Jesus blot out transgressions and clothe us with the robe of righteousness woven in the loom of heaven."—Ellen G. White, *Evangelism,* page 186.

"Because of the imputed righteousness of Christ they are accounted precious. . . . He (God the Father) does not see in them the vileness of the sinner. He recognizes in them the likeness of His Son, in whom they believe."—Ellen G. White, *The Desire of Ages,* page 667.

"There is . . . no condemnation to them which are in Christ Jesus, who walk not after the flesh, but after the Spirit." Romans 8:1.

We are blameless in God's sight, if we continue in the faith of Jesus. Philippians 2:15; Colossians 1:22, 23. We are perfect through Christ. Jesus' goodness is ours.

Justification by faith brings peace. "Therefore being justified by faith, we have peace with God through our Lord Jesus Christ: by whom also we have access by faith into this grace wherein we stand, and rejoice in hope of the glory of God." Romans 5:1, 2.

"And the work of righteousness shall be peace; and the effect of righteousness quietness and assurance forever." Isaiah 32:17.

Is Jesus your personal Saviour? Is your faith in Him solid? If so, God credits you with righteousness.

Be happy. All your sins are forgiven.

The Lord counts your faith as righteousness.

You are not condemned. In Christ, you have the peace of God.

Christ lives in you. Eternal life has already begun for you. In Him you have joy which will never end.

A person once said, "You Christians seem to have a religion that makes you miserable. You are like a man with a headache. He does not want to get rid of his head, but it hurts him to keep it."

Unhappy Christians have not met Christ, the happiness Jesus offers. He said: "These things have I spoken unto you, that My joy might remain in you, and that your joy might be full." John 15:11.

We are told to be happy. "Rejoice in the Lord alway: and again I say, Rejoice." Philippians 4:4.

With Christ living in you, every day can be a happy day. "The true, joyous life of the soul is to have Christ formed within."— Ellen G. White, *Steps to Christ,* page 47.

Many people are happy only when things go their way. If unfavorable things happen, they are unhappy. But Christ's goodness brings an inner abiding happiness, independent of external happenings.

"For I am convinced that nothing can ever separate us from His love. Death can't, and life can't. The angels won't, and all the powers of hell itself cannot keep God's love away. Our fears for today, our worries about tomorrow, or where we are—high above the sky, or in the deepest ocean—nothing will ever be able to separate us from the love of God demonstrated by our Lord Jesus Christ when He died for us." Romans 8:38, 39, Living Bible.

Christ within, gives life with a capital L. "He shall gain life who is justified through faith." Galatians 3:11, NEB.

The More Abundant Life

You will not find money between the pages of a book if no one ever placed it there. Many people want abundant life but can't find it because they are looking for it in places where it doesn't exist.

Nearly everybody thinks that the more abundant life comes through material prosperity. Three cars in every garage. A color TV in every room. Membership at the country club. A big bank account. Lots of cash around the house. Early retirement to a warm climate with no obligations to anybody or anything. Just take it easy and enjoy the reward of hard work.

The Bible says, "A man's life consisteth not in the abundance of the things which he possesseth." Luke 12:15. There is no real life in materialism. Recently fifty-four millionaires committed suicide in one year.

Jesus said, "I am ... the life." Without His life there is no living. Life at its best can be found only in Jesus Christ. "In Him was life; and the life was the light of men." John 1:4.

What is life without Christ? A newspaper once quoted various famous men on what life was. Marcus Aurelius said, "It's a battle." E. V. Cooke called it "a hollow bubble." Robert Browning: "an empty dream." Shakespeare: "a walking shadow." To John Gay it was "a jest." Amiel said it was "a document to be interpreted."

It was "a smoke that curls" to W. E. Henley. John Masefield described it as "a long headache in a noisy street." Napoleon thought it "a fortress which neither you nor I know anything about." For Bernard Shaw it was "a flame that is always burning itself out." Don Marquis saw it "like a scrambled egg."

Job said, "Man . . . is of few days, and full of trouble." Job 14:1. Solomon experimented with material pleasure. He wanted "to see what was that good for the sons of men, which they should do under heaven all the days of their life." He found that all things of the world ended in "vanity and vexation of spirit." Then he found that the best things in life are to fear God and keep His commandments. Ecclesiastes 2:3, 11; 12:13, 14. This is the key to real happiness.

Only Christ gives the more abundant life. He said, "I am come that they might have life, and that they might have it more abundantly." John 10:10.

The Spirit-filled life is the abundant and overflowing life. John 7:37-39. Christ living in the heart of the believer is the beginning of life everlasting.

"It is through the Spirit that Christ dwells in us; and the Spirit of God, received into the heart by faith, is the beginning of the life eternal."—Ellen G. White, *The Desire of Ages,* page 388.

Jesus' life is endless. So Christ in you is the beginning of eternal life.

Here is a list of the abundance God has for you, if you will accept Him into your life:

Abundant peace. "The peace of God, which passeth all understanding." "Thou will keep him in perfect peace, whose mind is stayed on Thee." Philippians 4:7; Isaiah 26:3.

Abundant joy. "That your joy might be full." "Your heart shall rejoice, and your joy no man taketh from you." John 15:11; 16:22.

Abundant love. "I have loved thee with an everlasting love." Jeremiah 31:3.

Abundant strength. "I can do all things through Christ which strengtheneth me." Philippians 4:13.

Abundant righteousness. "Being filled with the fruits of righteousness." Philippians 1:11.

Abundant pardon. "He will abundantly pardon." Isaiah 55:7.

Abundant grace. "God is able to make all grace abound toward you." 2 Corinthians 9:8.

Abundant satisfaction. "They shall be abundantly satisfied." Psalm 36:8.

Abundant power. God "is able to do exceeding abundantly above all that we ask or think, according to the power that worketh in us." Ephesians 3:20.

Abundant victory. "Thanks be unto God, which always causeth us to triumph in Christ." 2 Corinthians 2:14.

Abundant entrance into heaven. "An entrance shall be ministered unto you abundantly into the everlasting kingdom of our Lord and Saviour Jesus Christ." 2 Peter 1:11.

What a life Christ offers us! Abundant peace, joy, love, strength, grace, satisfaction, righteousness, pardon, power, victory, and immortality.

How can you have this? It is yours when you are in Christ and Christ is in you. Jesus revealed the secret in seven words—"Abide in Me, and I in you." John 15:4.

All of Christ's words and actions while on earth are the outward expression of the Father dwelling in Him. "The Father that dwelleth in Me, He doeth the works." John 14:10. This is the secret of His life. He depended completely upon the Father to speak and act through Him. He said, "I can of mine own self do nothing." John 5:30. His overflowing life was the result of His union with the Father.

We can have the same relationship with Him that He had with the Father. "As Thou hast sent Me into the world, even so have I also sent them into the world." John 17:18.

We receive the gift of the Holy Spirit, when we receive Christ. "Hereby know we that we dwell in Him, and He in us, because He hath given us of His Spirit." 1 John 4:13. "Hereby we know that He abideth in us, by the Spirit which He hath given us." 1 John 3:24.

Jesus said that He and the Father live in those who obey Him. John 14:23.

"He that dwelleth in love dwelleth in God, and God in him. *Herein is our love made perfect,* that we may have boldness in the day of judgment." 1 John 4:16, 17. We are perfected when Christ lives in us. Through Him we are transformed into His image.

Who Is a Jesus Person?

When we accept Christ, we accept Him for all that He is—what He taught and lived—what He said through His prophets and apostles. Romans 15:4; John 5:39. A Jesus person is one who accepts Jesus, and everything He is.

God says, "I, even I, am the Lord; and *beside Me there is no saviour.*" Isaiah 43:11.

Jesus said that He is the great I AM, or the self-existent One. John 8:58. Unless we accept Him, as the I AM, we will die in our sins and perish. John 8:24.

In the first chapter of John, Jesus is presented as the Eternal Word. "What God was, the Word [Christ] was." John 1:1, NEB. Christ's nature, essence, self-existence, and eternalness are one with the Father. He is God.

If we deny the deity and eternal preexistence of Christ, we reject Him. If Jesus were a created being, He could not have paid the price for sin. If we deny the virgin birth of Christ, we reject Him.

Honor Jesus as God the Son, self-existent and eternal with the Father. Honor Him as the second Person of the Godhead, with life original and unborrowed. Cherish Him as the Creator of all, who became the God-man, our only Saviour.

Accept His miraculous incarnation, His sinless life, His atoning death, His bodily resurrection, His ascension, and His priestly intercession in heaven. Accept His literal, visible, personal return to this earth, at the end of this age. Acts 1:9-11; Matthew 24:30.

When He comes, He will raise the righteous dead with immortal bodies. He will also change the living righteous from mortal to immortal. 1 Thessalonians 4:16, 17; 1 Corinthians 15:51-54. Then all the righteous from all generations will be gathered to the New Jerusalem in heaven. John 14:3; Matthew 24:30, 31.

One thousand years after this, Jesus will destroy the disobedient of all generations. He will reconstruct this earth, making it new and perfect. And His redeemed will then enjoy everlasting happiness. Revelation 20:7-15; 21:1; 2 Peter 3:10-13. You accept all this when you accept Christ.

Jesus regarded the Scriptures as the ultimate authority, as the final word in religion.

He quoted from Deuteronomy 8:3—"It is written, Man shall not live by bread alone, but by every word that proceedeth out of the mouth of God." Matthew 4:4. Jesus taught us to live by what the Scriptures say.

He taught that what the Scriptures say on any spiritual matter is final and must be believed and obeyed. Accepting Christ includes accepting the Word of God, the Bible, as our only guide in religion. But it cannot guide any of us if we don't read it. And if we don't obey it.

Jesus said, "Except a man be born again, he cannot see the kingdom of God." John 3:3. No one really accepts Christ unless he is born again.

The Holy Spirit, the third Person of the Godhead, is Christ's special Representative. Through the Spirit Jesus dwells in our heart. John 14:16-23. Accepting Christ includes receiving the Holy Spirit into your heart so Jesus can live through you.

If Christ lives in us, we will obey His commandments. This is the only way we can obey them. To accept Christ is to obey Him.

A real Jesus person obeys Jesus. John 14:15, 21, 23; 15:10. "Here is the test by which we can make sure that we know Him: do we keep His commands? The man who says, 'I know Him,' while he disobeys His commands, is a liar and a stranger to the truth." 1 John 2:3, 4, NEB.

"And to all He said, 'If anyone wishes to be a follower of Mine, he must leave self behind; *day after day he must take up his cross, and come with Me.*'" Luke 9:23, NEB. Paul expressed it this way: "I am crucified with Christ: nevertheless I live; yet not I, but Christ liveth in me." Galatians 2:20.

Accepting Jesus is a continual rejection of sin. It is constantly letting Christ live in us. Accepting Him is synonymous with obeying Him, believing on Him, following Him to the end.

Christ taught obedience to the Ten Commandments. Matthew 19:16-19. Jesus is the Creator. The Sabbath commandment identifies God as the Creator. So all ten are commandments of the Son of God, as much as they are commands of God the Father. Accepting Christ involves obedience to His law.

The fourth commandment from Christ is to keep holy the seventh day, Saturday. Obeying this Sabbath command is part of fully accepting Him. Jesus kept the day we call Saturday. The Romans ruled Palestine when He lived there. The seventh day of the week, which Jesus kept holy, was called the day of Saturn (or Saturday) by the Romans. The seventh-day Sabbath of the Ten Commandments is identical with the day of Saturn (or Saturday) which Jesus kept when He lived in Palestine.

The Bible says, "Jesus Christ the same yesterday, and today, and forever." Hebrews 13:8. He kept the seventh day. He attended divine worship on Saturday. He does not change. If He lived in your city as He once lived in Nazareth, He would keep Saturday and attend worship on this day. Keeping holy the seventh day, or Saturday, is a part of accepting Jesus.

"Ye should follow His steps." 1 Peter 2:21. Keeping the seventh day Sabbath, as specified in Jesus' commandments, is one of Christ's steps for us to follow.

The two greatest works of Christ in man's behalf are creation and redemption.

When He made this world, He set apart the seventh day as a special day for man—a memorial day to remind us that He is the

Creator. Compare Genesis 2:1-3 with Exodus 31:16, 17; 20:8-11. Since redemption is re-creation, Christ also appointed the seventh day to remind us that He is our Sanctifier. Ezekiel 20:12; Exodus 31:13. Christ's seventh-day Sabbath is a reminder that Jesus is the Creator-Redeemer. It is a link of love to draw us closer to Him, to help us know Him personally as an intimate friend.

(Those who may desire a fuller explanation of this, will find it in the sixty-four page booklet, "Link of Love," also published by Pacific Press Publishing Association.)

You may not be aware of the necessity of honoring Christ's Sabbath. You may think that keeping Sunday in honor of His resurrection on the first day of the week is accepting Christ. But search your Bible. You will find that neither Christ nor His apostles ever instructed Christians to keep Sunday. Accept Christ all the way. Observe His Sabbath.

Jesus taught tithing. Paying one-tenth of our net income, for the support of God's work. He mentioned how particular the Pharisees were in tithing. They even paid tithe on the small herbs in their gardens. But at the same time they "omitted the weightier matters of the law, judgment, mercy, and faith." Christ said they should be just, merciful, and faithful, as well as tithe payers. "These ought ye to have done," He said, "and not to leave the other undone." Matthew 23:23. A full commitment to Christ includes paying tithe.

To accept Christ we must believe what He taught about death. He showed that all the unjust will be cast into the lake of fire at the same time on the final day of judgment. Matthew 13:49, 50; Revelation 20:12-15. He said that this fire will wipe them out soul and body. Matthew 10:28; Malachi 4:1-3.

Jesus said that all the righteous of all generations will go to heaven on the same day when He comes the second time. Matthew 24:30, 31. The main reason for His second coming is to take all the obedient to the mansions in heaven. John 14:3. The righteous do not go to heaven until He comes again.

Jesus taught that no one receives a reward until He comes again. Matthew 16:27; 25:31-46; Luke 14:14.

Jesus taught that death is a sleep. John 11:11, 14. Since the dead are asleep, they "know not anything." Ecclesiastes 9:5. Their power to think has perished. Psalm 146:3, 4.

Jesus said the dead cannot live again until they are resurrected. John 5:28, 29. He said that not one who accepted Him would be lost, but all who love Him will be raised when He comes. John 6:39, 40.

What Jesus taught concerning the hereafter is the truth. When we accept Him, we also accept His teachings about death.

He showed that accepting Him involves rejecting all sin. His followers are not part of this world, even as He was not of it. John 17:15; 15:19. He calls us to reject unbelief and sin. "Be ye separate, saith the Lord, and touch not the unclean." 2 Corinthians 6:17.

Jesus inaugurated the ordinance of the broken bread and the consecrated unfermented wine. Observing this Last Supper reveals faith in His sacrifice. It reminds us that His body was broken for us and His blood was shed for our sins. Matthew 26:26-28.

When He instituted the Lord's Supper, He instituted the ordinance of foot-washing to show our love for one another—to remind us to be unselfish in serving others. John 13:1-15. When Peter refused to have his feet washed, Jesus said, "If I wash thee not, thou hast no part with Me." John 13:8. If we want a part with Christ, we must obey Him. Regardless of how unimportant a certain thing may seem, if Christ has commanded it, then it is part of accepting Him.

"He that believeth and *is baptized* shall be saved." Jesus said. Mark 16:16. "Go ye therefore, and teach all nations, *baptizing them* in the name of the Father, and of the Son, and of the Holy Ghost." Matthew 28:19.

He made it plain that this baptism is by immersion. In Mark 1:9, 10, we are told that Jesus was baptized *in* the river Jordan. He was lowered under water when He was baptized. He came "up out of the water," afterwards. This is the example He left us. We "should follow His steps." 1 Peter 2:21.

We are to be buried with Christ in baptism and rise with Him.

Colossians 2:12. Immersion portrays burial and resurrection. It is Christ's appointed way for us to show our faith in His death, burial, and resurrection. Romans 6:3-5. It is part of accepting Christ.

In Revelation 12:17 Jesus says that the last segment of His church will be distinguished by keeping His commandments, and having His testimony. The testimony of Jesus is "the spirit of prophecy." Revelation 19:10. So a part of accepting Jesus is accepting His testimony, as presented by the spirit of prophecy. And this spirit of prophecy is found in His remnant church, a group of Christians who keep His commandments.

Do you want to find this remnant church, this group of believers who love and obey Christ? They are known as Seventh-day Adventists. They accept Christ's way completely.

The wisest, best, and safest course for each of us is to follow the Lord Jesus all the way. Few of us have fully accepted Christ. A partial acceptance is good, but it does not go far enough.

Christ said, "So likewise, whosoever he be of you that forsaketh not all that he hath, he cannot be My disciple." Luke 14:33. None of us can fully accept Christ until we completely surrender to Him. We must reject everything that is contrary to His teachings. We must comply with all that He has commanded. A real Jesus person makes this full commitment to the Saviour.

Accept Christ completely. Then you can say with joy, "For me to live is Christ." Philippians 1:21.

Are You Saved?

We are all individuals. Yet each of us is identical in the need for Christ and the salvation He offers. To be saved is our greatest need.

"For what is a man profited, if he shall gain the whole world, and lose his own soul?" Matthew 16:26.

Your salvation is worth more than all the money, gold, diamonds, houses, lands, factories, railroads, airplanes, and automobiles in the world.

The Bible tells us how to be saved, and how we may be sure of salvation. 2 Timothy 3:15.

Only Christ can save us. Acts 4:12. Salvation is His gift which we receive through faith in Him.

We cannot earn it. "For by grace are ye saved through faith; and that not of yourselves: it is the gift of God: not of works, lest any man should boast." Ephesians 2:8, 9.

Salvation comes when we receive Christ as our personal Saviour. Acts 16:30, 31. We are saved through Him.

Jesus stressed, "He that shall endure unto the end, the same shall be saved." Matthew 24:13. Those who are not true to Christ cannot be saved. "Be thou faithful unto death, and I will give thee a crown of life." Revelation 2:10. "For we are made partakers of Christ, if we hold the beginning of our confidence steadfast unto the end." Hebrews 3:14.

Life has three dimensions—past, present, and future. Salvation also has past, present, and future dimensions. God offers complete salvation.

Paul speaks of a threefold deliverance in Christ. A past, present, and future salvation. "Who delivered us from so great a death, and doth deliver: in whom we trust that He will yet deliver us." 2 Corinthians 1:10.

What kind of a salvation do we need? *First,* we need to be saved from the guilt and penalty of our sins. *Second,* we need His salvation every day from the domination and control of our sinful nature. *Third,* beyond this life we need to be saved in heaven from all the effects of sin, from the presence of sin, and from the possibility of sinning. God has met these three needs through Jesus Christ.

In 2 Timothy 1:9 we read that God *"hath saved us."* In Romans 8:24 the Word says that we *"are saved"* (*"have been saved,"* NEB; *"were saved,"* RSV).

These scriptures refer to the salvation we have when we receive Christ as our personal Saviour. At that time we are saved from the guilt and punishment of our past sins.

Christ told a sinful woman, "Thy sins are forgiven." Then He said, "Thy faith *hath saved* thee." Luke 7:48, 50. He did not say, "Thy faith will save thee." Or "thy faith is saving thee." But "thy faith *hath saved* thee." She had been saved from the guilt of her past sins.

Then there was Zacchaeus. He received Christ not merely as a guest in his home, but as his Saviour. So Jesus said, "This day is salvation come to this house." Luke 19:9.

Jesus said that anyone who believes on Him "hath everlasting life, and shall not come into condemnation; but *is passed* from death unto life." John 5:24.

The apostle John declared: "We know that we *have passed* from death unto life, because we love the brethren." 1 John 3:14. Notice he does not say that the born-again believer may pass, or will pass, from death to life, but he *has passed* from death unto life.

The Bible not only speaks of born-again believers as those who have been saved, but also as *those who are being saved.* In Acts 2:47 Christians are spoken of as "those whom He was saving" (NEB), or "those who were being saved" (RSV). "To us who are being saved." 1 Corinthians 1:18, RSV. This aspect of salvation is accomplished daily as Christ lives His life in the born-again believer. Galatians 2:20.

A pardoned sinner does not have within himself the power to live a good life. When he receives salvation from the guilt and penalty of his past sins, immediately he needs to be saved from the dominion or power of sin. So Christ provides day-by-day salvation by continually giving us His own goodness. Christ lives in us and gives us power to obey.

Imputed righteousness saves from the guilt, defilement, and penalty of sin. Imparted righteousness saves from the power and dominion of sin day by day. The first is the remedy for sinful actions. The second provides victory over our sinful nature.

Some come to Christ and are converted. They make a good start. They have a salvation that takes care of their sinful past. But they don't move forward. They don't abide in Christ each day, allowing Him to change their natures.

Many of us do not appreciate the gift of Christ's righteousness. This gift keeps us each day from the power of sin. We must abide in Christ for complete salvation.

Some think that the Ten Commandments no longer bind one who has received Christ. We cannot save ourselves by obeying the law. But Christ saves us from our sins and enables us to obey the commandments.

Disobeying the Ten Commandments is sin. 1 John 3:4; Romans 7:7. No one is saved if he intentionally disobeys this law. "For as we willfully persist in sin after receiving the knowledge of the truth, no sacrifice for sins remains." Hebrews 10:26, NEB.

God is fair and loving. His law of the Ten Commandments is fair. It proceeds from His love. And our love is expressed by obedience.

Believers are saved not only when they receive Christ. They are not only being saved as Christ lives in them each day, but they will also be saved eternally at the second coming of Christ. "So Christ was once offered to bear the sins of many; and unto them that look for Him shall He appear the second time without sin unto salvation." Hebrews 9:28.

This final phase of salvation, this third dimension, is accomplished at Christ's second advent.

When Christ comes, He will call the righteous dead to life. He will change both the righteous dead and the righteous living into immortality. And they will never die again. All the righteous who have ever lived on earth will go to heaven with Jesus. Matthew 24:30, 31; John 14:3; 1 Thessalonians 4:16, 17.

God has provided a complete and permanent solution to our sin problem.

Accept, love, and obey Jesus. Then you can say, "I have been saved from the guilt and penalty of my sins by receiving Jesus as my personal Saviour. I am being saved from the power of sin by Jesus living in me each day. And I expect that when He comes again, I shall be saved from the very presence and possibility of sin."

Solved Forever

Redemption saves not only the soul, but also our bodies. Sin physically weakens us and brings death. The Bible speaks of "the redemption of our body." Romans 8:23. This happens when Christ comes again. Then all the righteous, who have ever lived, will receive sinless, immortal bodies, forever free from death and sickness. 1 Corinthians 15:51-55; Philippians 3:20, 21.

After a thousand years those who hate God will be destroyed forever. Every trace of sin will be wiped away. God will reconstruct this earth into a perfect new earth. Revelation 21:1-5; 22:3, 4. The earth itself is suffering from the effects of sin now. Isaiah 24:5, 6. But God will change that. Then "there shall be no more curse." No more sorrow, sickness, pain, or death.

Those who let Christ solve their sin problem will inherit this perfect new earth. 2 Peter 3:10-13; Matthew 5:5. "And the ransomed of the Lord shall return, and come to Zion with songs and everlasting joy upon their heads: they shall obtain joy and gladness, and sorrow and sighing shall flee away." Isaiah 35:10.

Then God's purpose will be fulfilled. Sin will not rise up the second time to mar the perfect harmony of the universe. Nahum 1:9. The entire problem is settled forever.

Lucifer's rebellion tore apart the perfect harmony of the universe. Christ's object is to restore that harmony. His sacrifice will end sin forever. Daniel 9:24. The cross was Satan's knell. Hebrews 2:14.

The cross not only reconciled us to God; it also prepared the way for restoring complete harmony in the entire universe. "Through Him [Christ] God chose to reconcile the whole universe to Himself, making peace through the shedding of His blood upon the cross—to reconcile all things, whether on earth or in heaven, through Him alone." Colossians 1:20, NEB.

Through Christ "He has made known to us His hidden purpose—such was His will and pleasure determined beforehand in Christ—to be put into effect when the time was ripe: namely, that the universe, all in heaven and on earth, might be brought into a unity in Christ." Ephesians 1:9, 10, NEB.

Revelation, the last book in the Bible, closes with the fulfillment of God's purpose. The plan, which He and His Son laid for us in pre-creation days, will be fully accomplished.

In the new earth, God will have a perfect world filled with perfect people who will enjoy perfect happiness for all eternity. He will have what He planned for.

"And every creature which is in heaven, and on the earth, and under the earth, and such as are in the sea, and all that are in them, heard I saying, Blessing, and honor, and glory, and power, be unto Him that sitteth upon the throne, and unto the Lamb forever and ever." Revelation 5:13.

Accept God's solution for your sin problem. Accept, and rejoice. Because a whole new world awaits you.